I'M NOT A FEMINIST

CHRISTINE ROCHE

CHRISTINE ROCHE was born in Montreal, Quebec, in 1939. She has lived
in London since 1969. In the early '70s she became involved in film
animation and agitprop as a freelance illustrator and cartoonist. Her
work has appeared in many publications, and versions of some of these
illustrations have been published in: *Danger! Men at Work* Rosalind Miles
(Futura), *Pictures of Women: Sexuality* Jane Root (Pandora), *New
Statesman, New Society, City Limits, Feminist Review,* and pamphlets and
posters for the NCCL, NATPHE and NUJ.

Published by VIRAGO PRESS Limited 1985
41 William IV Street, London WC2N 4DB

British Library Cataloguing in Publication Data

Roche, Christine
  I'm not a feminist, but–.
  1. Canadian wit and humor, Pictorial
  I. Title
  741.5'971   NC1449

  ISBN 0-86068-604-3

Printed in Great Britain by Whitstable Litho
at Whitstable, Kent

Behind every great man...
MIRACLE!
MIRACLE!
BRAVO!
MIRACLE!
BRAVO!
BRAVO!
MIRACLE
MIRACLE

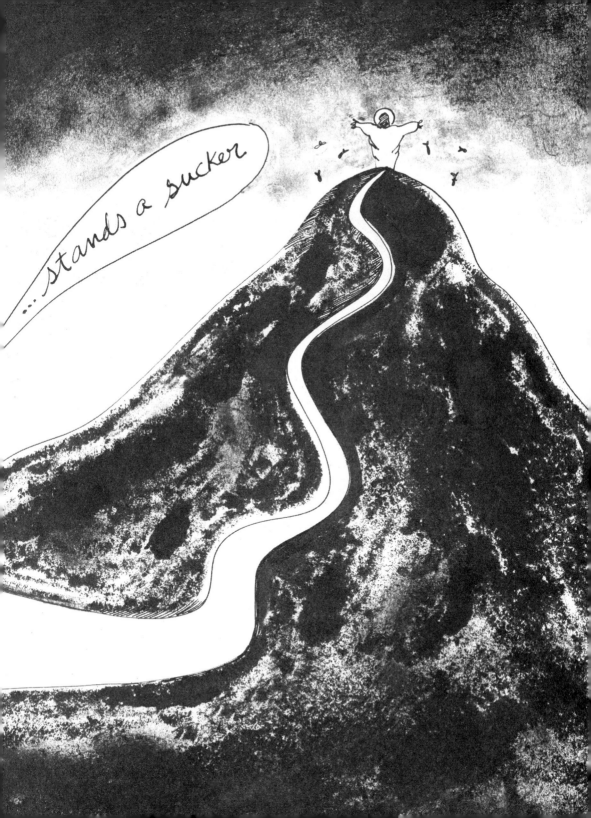

Hack Street

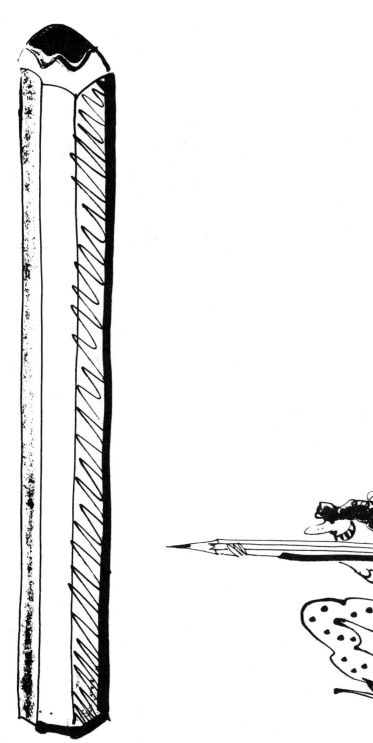

DR. WOLF.

WHAT DO YOU
MEAN -
OPPRESSED -
I DO IT
BECAUSE
i WANT to.

DR. LAMB

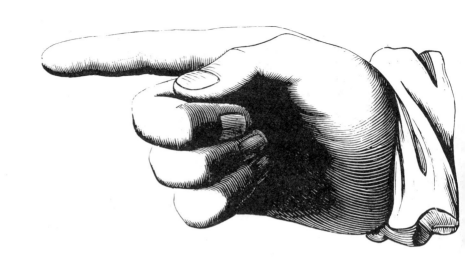

WOMEN
HAVE
NO
SENSE
OF
HUMOUR.

DR. WOLF

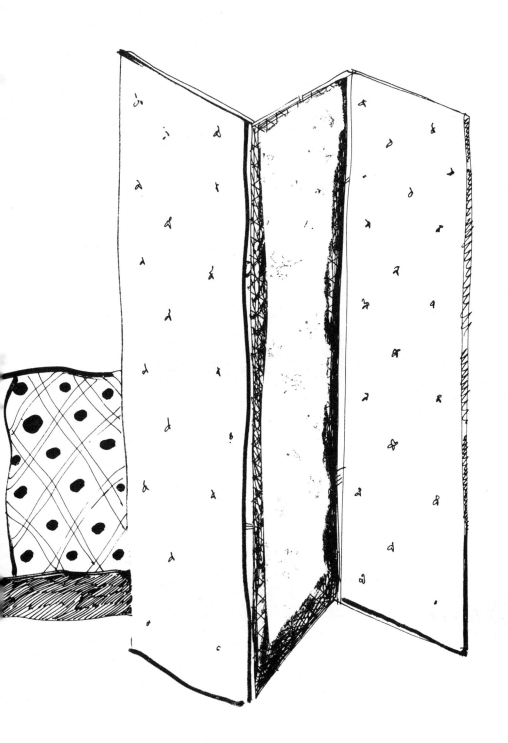

EN FAMILLE.

we're all
butterflies
under
the skin
Doreen,
All
butterflies...

pterodactyls,
smart ass —
pterodactyls.

I FEEL THAT SOMETIMES YOU'RE TAKING ME OVER.

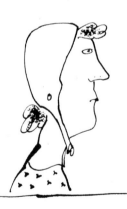

thank you.

...AGE 45...
TIRED.... THE OCCASIONAL
HEADACHE....
BETTER HAVE THE
OPERATION.
IT'LL MAKE YOU
FEEL LIKE A NEW MAN-
AND SAVE US A LOT
OF TROUBLE.

DR. LAMB

I KNOW
WHICH SIDE
MY BREAD
IS
BUTTERED
ON.

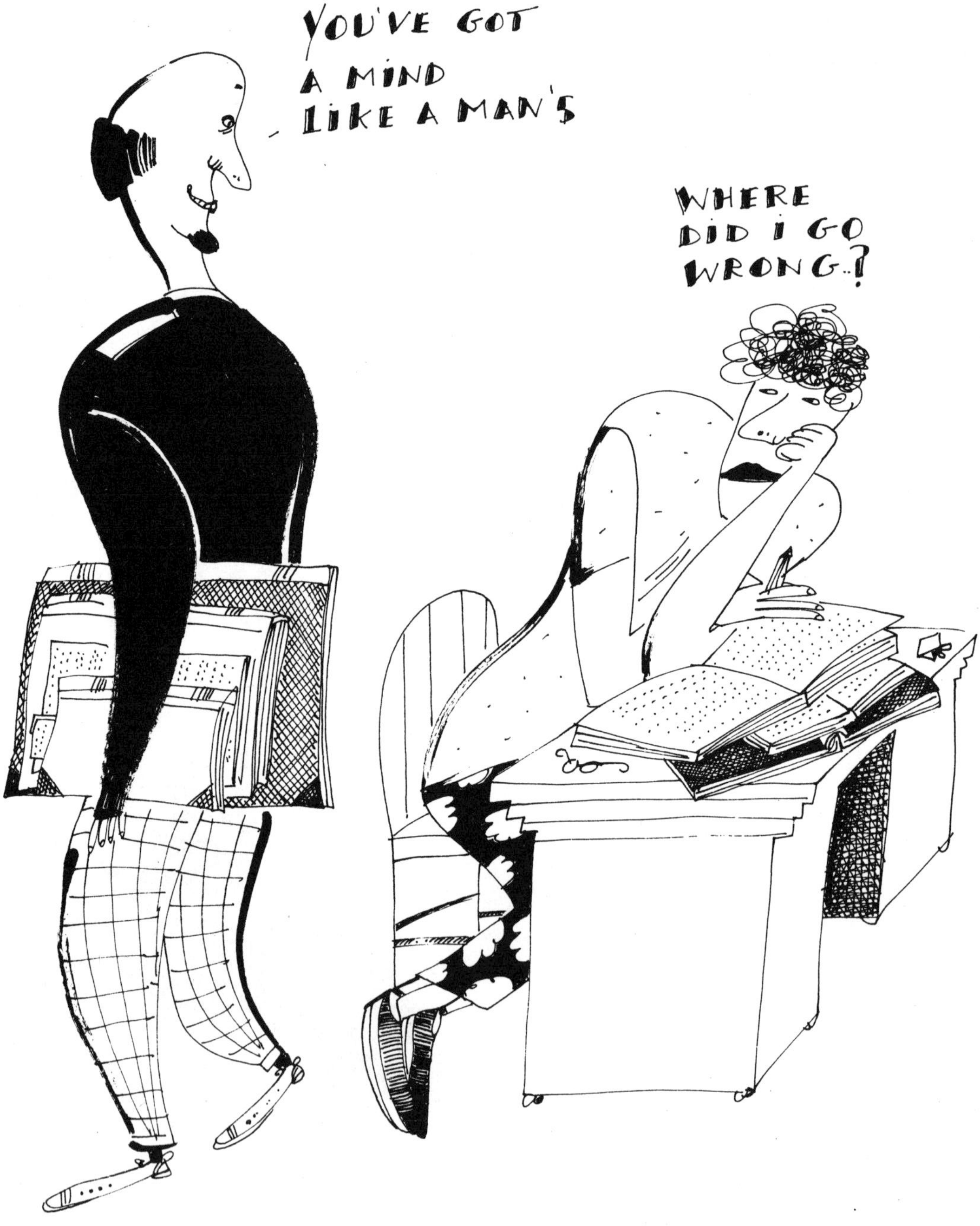
YOU'VE GOT A MIND LIKE A MAN'S
WHERE DID I GO WRONG..?

ARE YOU MARRIED OR ANYTHING ?
YES - ANYTHING -
TWO WAY MIRRORS, WHIPS, LEATHER, THE LOT.
WHAT ABOUT YOU ?
PERSONNEL

THE FIFTH COLUMNIST

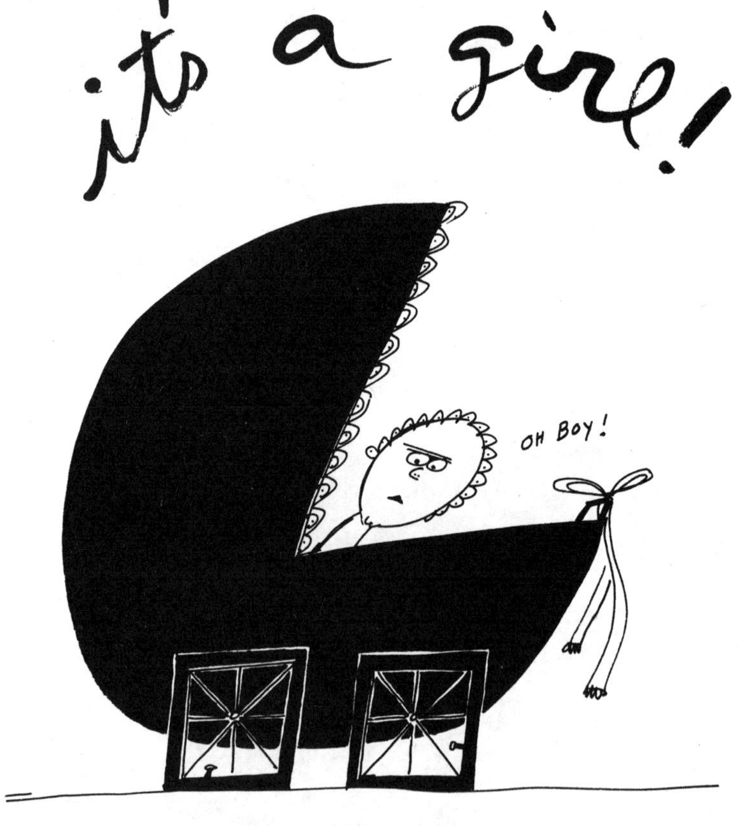
it's a girl!
OH BOY!

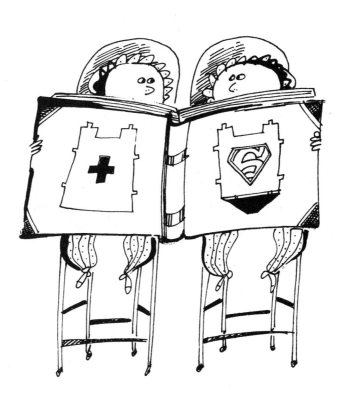

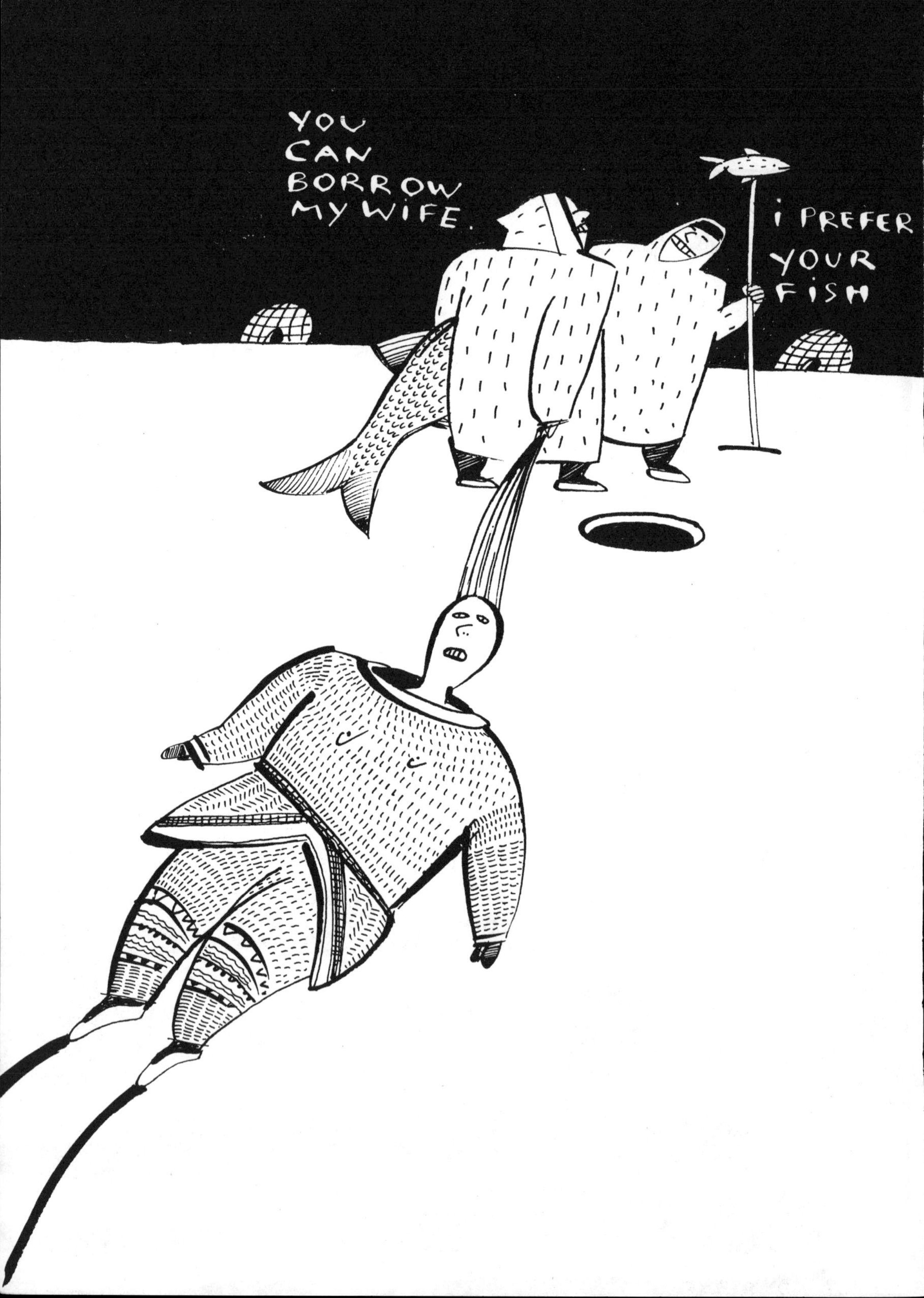
YOU CAN BORROW MY WIFE.
I PREFER YOUR FISH

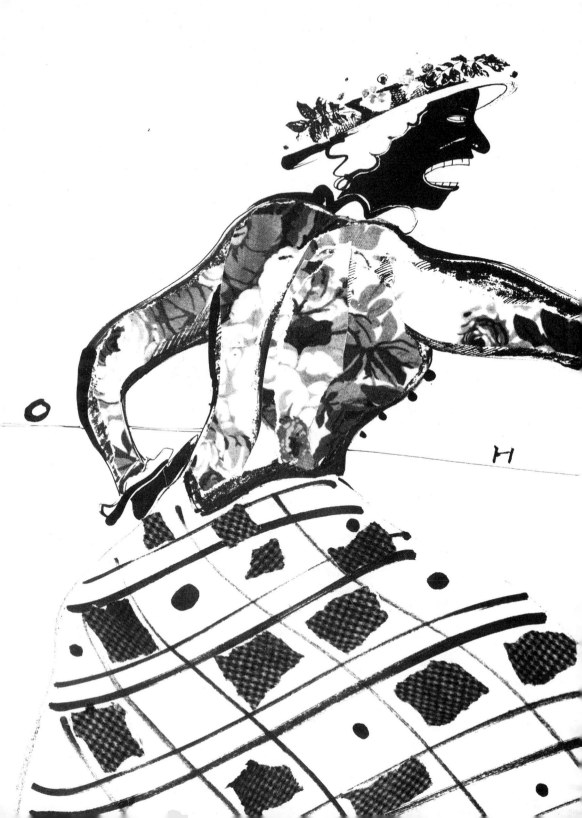

SOJOURNER TRUTH, EX-SLAVE AND VETERAN
FEMINIST AND ABOLITIONIST CAMPAIGNER,
ANSWERED A MALE HECKLER AT A WOMEN'S
RIGHTS MEETING IN AKRON, OHIO, IN 1851:

"THE MAN OVER THERE SAYS
WOMEN NEED TO BE HELPED
INTO CARRIAGES AND LIFTED
OVER DITCHES. NOBODY EVER
HELPS ME INTO CARRIAGES
OR OVER PUDDLES—
AND AIN'T I A WOMAN?
LOOK AT MY ARM! I'VE
PLOUGHED AND PLANTED AND
NO MAN COULD HEAD ME—
AND AIN'T I A WOMAN?"

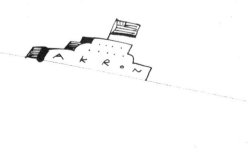

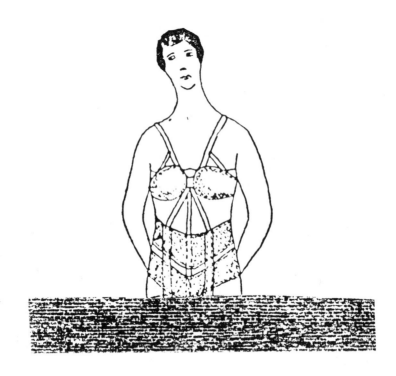

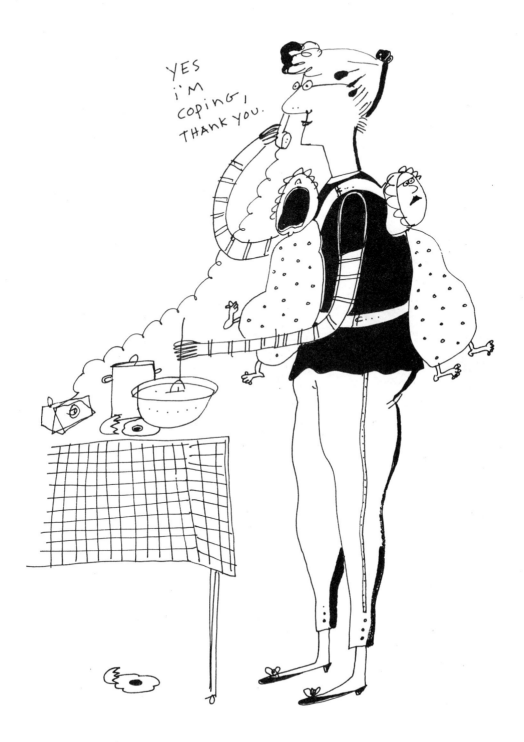

NOW BE
CREATIVE

Iceberg, most of it submerged

THE MODERN THEORY OF THE DESCENT OF MAN

ALL Lies...